IMAGES
of America

HISTORIC SIGNS OVER
CALIFORNIA'S ROADWAYS

Merced had two "Gateway to Yosemite" signs. The one seen above stretched over old US Highway 99 on Sixteenth Street at G Street, which at the time was the northern edge of the city. The other sign, on the southern city limit, is pictured on page 82. Both concrete signs were erected in 1927. The letters on the signs were one foot high and ringed by neon tubing.

ON THE COVER: Santa Rosa had an overhead sign with "Santa Rosa" on one side and "Redwood Highway" on the other. Both sides of the sign can be seen on page 67. The sign was over Mendocino Avenue on the route of the old Redwood Highway. The Redwood Highway stretches from San Francisco to Del Norte County on what is now US Highway 101. (Courtesy of the Sonoma County Library.)

IMAGES
of America

HISTORIC SIGNS OVER
CALIFORNIA'S ROADWAYS

Michael Lynch and Arthur Sommers

ARCADIA
PUBLISHING

Published by Arcadia Publishing
Charleston, South Carolina

Printed in the United States of America

Library of Congress Control Number: 2021947612

For all general information, please contact Arcadia Publishing:
Telephone 843-853-2070
Fax 843-853-0044
E-mail sales@arcadiapublishing.com
For customer service and orders:
Toll-Free 1-888-313-2665

Visit us on the Internet at www.arcadiapublishing.com

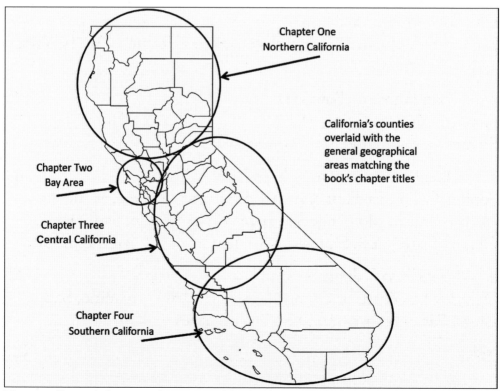

Chapter One
Northern California

California's counties
overlaid with the
general geographical
areas matching the
book's chapter titles

Chapter Two
Bay Area

Chapter Three
Central California

Chapter Four
Southern California

This map illustrates the geographic areas used for the chapters in this book. (Courtesy of the authors.)

CONTENTS

ACKNOWLEDGMENTS

Special thanks are extended to Brian Smith and Rodi Lee for editing this book. A valuable source for this project was Bernard C. Winn's 1993 book *Arch Rivals—90 Years of Welcome Arches in Small-Town America*. Most images contained in this book were acquired by author Michael Lynch (mike.lynch.signs@gmail.com) over more than two decades. Many of these images are from vintage postcards, old prints, and research sources like libraries, history museums, and historical societies. Nearly all the modern images are from photographs taken by Michael Lynch during one of his many trips throughout California. Unless otherwise noted, all images appear courtesy of the authors. This book is sponsored by the Placer County Historical Foundation, and all authors' royalties from the book are being donated directly to the foundation.

An elaborate wood-and-plaster 40-foot-high arch sign was temporarily erected in 1907 for the Lodi Tokay Grape Carnival. Located at Pine and Sacramento Streets, the sign was the focal point for the estimated 40,000 visitors to the carnival. This arched sign is mentioned in the introduction and also appears on page 80, where it is framed by an arch also constructed in 1907.

INTRODUCTION

This book is a photographic history of overhanging signs above roadways in California. The book contains over 220 images of such signs in over 150 locations. The authors have identified more than 300 historic overhead signs in California, although images or good images do not exist for all of them.

The earliest known images of such signs come from San Francisco and date from the Civil War era. See pages 61 and 62 for images of those early signs.

Prior to 1900, most arch signs were celebratory "parade"-type signs temporarily constructed for use during holidays or significant events. Many of these parade arches were extremely elaborate and both provided a welcome and acted as a backdrop for parades and processions. The Native Sons of the Golden West (NSGW) were particularly involved in constructing parade arches for Independence Day and California Admission Day celebrations. Parade arches continued to be used well into the first half of the 20th century. One of the most elaborate parade arches constructed after 1900 was at the 1907 Tokay Festival in Lodi. An estimated 40,000 people attended the event, and most would have gone under the arch many times during the weeklong festivities.

The golden era of arch and overhead hanging signs started after 1900 and was associated with the traveling public. The first of these signs were near railway stations, but later they were almost exclusively linked to the era of automobile travel. At this time, electricity became available to many areas, and lighted signs, often spelling out the name of the community, became popular. Also during this period, there seems to have been a competition between many communities either to have a sign or to have one more elaborate than other communities. Numerous signs were constructed during this era throughout the state.

The decline of arch and overhead signs began in the late 1940s and continued into the 1950s and 1960s. During this time, there was major funding to improve roads and to build highways and freeways. Arch-type signs, with their narrow span widths, were particularly vulnerable to being removed for road-widening projects.

Fortunately, not all of the historic arch and overhead hanging signs were taken down. A fair number still exist and can still be seen today.

A wonderful revival of arch signs began in the 1980s. The most extensive return of arch signs occurred in San Diego when, starting in the early 1980s, ten different neighborhood arch signs were erected. This trend of new arch signs is still in full swing, with several new arch signs being proposed and/or constructed each year. The authors have identified over 100 modern arch signs currently in California.

The book is organized into four chapters, one for each region of California, as seen on the map on the page 4. These regions are Northern California, the San Francisco Bay Area, Central California, and Southern California. Within the chapters, the images are arranged in alphabetical order. An index is provided at the end of the book listing all the community signs alphabetically on a statewide basis.

On the following page are images from Watsonville and Ben Lomond that are good examples of historic overhead roadway signs.

Watsonville's "The Apple City—Santa Cruz County" sign is pictured here in 1926. The letters of the sign are lit by lightbulbs. The sign is on old California Highway 1 (Main Street) on the city's southern boundary at the Pajero River. Watsonville is still famous for the apples grown in the area but is also a major growing area for berries and other crops.

Ben Lomond's simple hanging sign is a classic design of the 1920–1930s, with just the letters of the community lit by lightbulbs. It appears to be on Main Street. Ben Lomond is located on California Highway 9 about 12 miles from Santa Cruz in Santa Cruz County.

One

NORTHERN CALIFORNIA

AMADOR, BUTTE, COLUSA, DEL NORTE, EL DORADO, GLENN, HUMBOLDT, LAKE, LASSEN, MENDOCINO, MODOC, NEVADA, PLACER, PLUMAS, SACRAMENTO, SHASTA, SIERRA, SISKIYOU, SUTTER, TEHAMA, TRINITY, YOLO, AND YUBA COUNTIES

In Auburn, Placer County, at the end of the 19th century, Jacob Roll had a five-acre orchard he called Uplands at the intersection of High Street with Sacramento Street. Roll's property was on High Street near the entrance to Auburn's Gold Country Fairgrounds. (Courtesy of Gene Dahlberg.)

A parade enters Auburn's Gold County Fairgrounds under a wooden arch with painted panels in the 1960s. The wooden arch was set onto stone pillars constructed by the Great Depression era's Works Progress Administration (WPA) in 1940. The wooden arch was taken down after it suffered damage from a large truck making a delivery. (Courtesy of Placer County Museums.)

A new metal arch was installed in 2017 atop the 1940 WPA-constructed pillars at the entrance to the Auburn Gold County Fairgrounds. A second fairgrounds arch sign can be seen farther down the road. There is one other modern fairground arch sign (not pictured). Auburn has two other modern arches, one at the high school and one at the entrance to Dingus McGee's Roadhouse.

The Big Bend campground sign is porcelain enamel. Big Bend is in the Tahoe National Forest on the South Yuba River in Placer County. The Lincoln Highway and historic US Highway 40 passed in front of the campground and nearby ranger station. Overland Emigrant Trail California Historical Landmark No. 799-2 marks where the first emigrants to cross the Sierra Nevada wintered in 1844–1845. (Courtesy of Placer County Museums.)

The McArthur-Burney overhead park entrance sign was constructed by the Civilian Conservation Corps (CCC) in 1934. The CCC worked in McArthur-Burney Falls Memorial State Park from 1934 to 1937. The park, in Shasta County, was established in 1926. It is best known for the 129-foot-tall Burney Falls, which has a constant flow of more than 100 million gallons per day. It is located on California Highway 89.

Cal-Neva was a resort and casino straddling the border between California and Nevada. It was built on the north shore of Lake Tahoe in 1926. The resort attracted famous people, which greatly increased when Frank Sinatra and Dean Martin bought into the resort in 1960. It has been closed since 2013. The property's current owner is billionaire Larry Ellison, who is a cofounder of Oracle Corporation.

Camp Sacramento, owned by the City of Sacramento, is a family camp and conference center that has been operating since 1920. It is located on US Highway 50 near the small town of Twin Bridges in El Dorado County. Sacramento (90 miles west of the camp) leases the land from El Dorado National Forest. Frank Williams built the bridge across the south fork of the American River into the camp area in the 1920s.

The "Choose Chico" lighted sign, partially obscured by the replica of the Liberty Bell, was dedicated on March 29, 1915. It was located on Fifth Street at the Southern Pacific Railroad depot. The sign was purchased and installed by the Chico Development Committee. The replica Liberty Bell was on its way to the 1915 San Francisco Panama-Pacific International Exposition. (Courtesy of Chico State University.)

Corning's overhead sign was erected in 1907, at the time the city was incorporated. The electrically illuminated letters on the sign spell out "Corning—The Clean Town," referring to the city's prohibition against alcohol sales. The sign was located on Solano Street on old US Highway 99. Formerly called Riceville, the area was home to the Maywood Colony, founded in 1891.

In 1924, the slogan on the bottom of the Corning sign was changed to "The Olive Town." Corning is recognized as the table olive capital of the United States and the second largest producer in the world after Spain. The sign was taken down in the 1930s.

This is the Breakers Motor Apartments arch sign in Crescent City. Crescent City is the county seat of Del Norte County and is named for the crescent-shaped stretch of beach on the Pacific Ocean. In 1964, a disastrous tidal wave struck the city, and afterward, a metal sign was hung across US Highway 101 proclaiming Crescent City "Come Back Town USA." No photographs of this sign are known to exist.

The University of California, Davis, celebrates an annual Picnic Day, and this is the entry arch for the 1915 celebration. This type of temporary arch, made from hay bales, was a common method of construction in the early years of Picnic Day. The Picnic Day tradition started in 1909 and is still held annually. (Courtesy of John Lofland.)

This elaborate archway entrance to the city of Davis was completed at Second and G Streets in 1916. It was removed in 1924 over concerns of automobile traffic safety. The small sign on left arch says: "Gateway to Yolo County," and the one on the right says: "Home of University Farms." The Davis Women's Improvement Club raised much of the funds needed to erect the arch. (Courtesy of John Lofland.)

Donner Lake Camp was a vintage resort area operated by Wally Gelatt at the western end of Donner Lake and is not to be confused with the Donner Memorial State Park, located at the eastern end of Donner Lake. Donner Lake is near the town of Truckee in Nevada County.

The Duncan Mineral Springs arch sign also has a square sign reading "AAA—American Automobile Association—Official" hanging below the crossbeam indicating it was listed in the AAA guide at the time. The area had been a hot springs resort by the early 1880s. The image is from the 1920s or early 1930s. Later, this Mendocino County area shortened its name to just Duncan Springs.

Shasta Retreat is a resort on Scarlett Way within the city limits of Dunsmuir on old US Highway 99. This postcard photograph was taken in 1941. Dunsmuir, in Siskiyou County, historically was a railroad town and popular vacation destination due to its mineral springs, waterfalls, and the Sacramento River flowing through the area. The resort fronted old US Highway 99.

This arched welcome sign was erected over the entrance to a Dunsmuir motel named Shasta Springs Motel. The picture was taken in 1948. This was one of many motels that sprang up during the 1930s and 1940s to cater to tourists motoring to or through the area on old US Highway 99.

Grass Valley celebrated California's 50th anniversary of statehood by raising a large statue-like miner welcome arch over the entrance to Mill Street and another at the entrance to Main Street in 1900. This sign was at Main and Auburn Streets. The town also had a "Welcome to Grass Valley" sign in the 1930s over Main Street. Two of the richest hard-rock gold mines in California, the Empire Mine and the North Star Mine, are in the Grass Valley area of Nevada County. California Highway 49 originally was routed through the middle of town. (Courtesy of Jim Johnson.)

The entry arch into the Jackson Rancheria Resort was erected in 2006 as part of the hotel, casino, and resort development. The resort is owned and operated by the Jackson Rancheria band of Miwuk Indians. The band was first recognized by the federal government in 1898. The resort is on the outskirts of Jackson on US Highway 50. Jackson is the county seat of Amador County.

This simple sign was strung over what was then Lincoln Highway (later US Highway 40), which passed through Loomis. It was lit by a light shining down on the sign. Namesake James Loomis was a saloon keeper, railroad agent, express agent, and postmaster. Early in the 20th century, Loomis was the second largest fruit-shipping station in Placer County. Loomis finally incorporated as a town in 1984.

In 1911, Marysville in Yuba County erected seven large lit arches over First Street. Reportedly, hundreds turned out for the lighting of the arches. Due to poor maintenance, all the arches were torn down in 1924 and 1925. They did not have signs on them but supported streetlights and the overhead electric power lines for the interurban trolley system. One arch was given to Rio Linda in Sacramento County.

A campaign was initiated in Marysville to resurrect the arches in the old downtown area. The first new arch, built at Fifth and D Streets, was dedicated in 1996. There are now arches at Third, Fourth, Fifth, and Sixth and D Streets. The new arches are illuminated, have a streetlight and flagpole in the center, and are used for temporary signs.

By 1922, Mount Shasta City had its new name (its previous name was Sisson), and in 1923, the chamber of commerce authorized an entry sign to be built on US Highway 99, the main street of the town. This photograph was taken in December 1931. The sign was removed by 1940. Mount Shasta City is in Siskiyou County about nine miles from the 14,179-foot-high Mount Shasta, the fifth highest peak in California.

North Highlands in Sacramento County was home to the former McClellan Air Force Base. Since decommissioning in 2009, it is now home to hundreds of private companies and state, federal, and local government agencies. This is one of two modern arch signs at the former main gate off Watt Avenue. The former airbase is now known as McClellan Business Park.

Orland sits on old US Highway 99 in Glenn County. This vintage photograph was taken some time after the archway's completion in 1926 over the highway at the north entrance to the town. The 43-foot-wide and 18-foot-high sign is made from steel, concrete, and stucco. In 2017, Orland proclaimed itself the "Queen Bee Capital of North America" owing to its robust local and regional queen honeybee production.

The sign at Orland's city limits was renovated in 2009 to honor the city's 100-year anniversary. Over time, the sign has had different wording on it, including "Welcome—Shop" in the 1950s. An approximately half-sized replica pedestrian version of the arch was constructed at the entrance to the city's Library Park in 2002.

The NSGW sponsored this parade arch erected on Montgomery Street in Oroville in 1900. This is one of three arches constructed for what was probably California's 50-year anniversary of statehood. This one was titled the Patriotic Arch. It was decorated in red, white, and blue and studded with lights. Oroville is the county seat of Butte County.

Oroville's Feather River sign at Riverbend Park was constructed in 2006. The 210-acre park is sandwiched between the Feather River and California Highway 70. It is just one of 15 facilities operated by the Feather River Recreation and Park District. There is another simple overhead sign at the entrance to the district's Berry Creek Park, which opened in 2014.

Placerville held a Fourth of July parade in 1896 down the city's Main Street. Placerville was once known as Hangtown in the early Gold Rush days. California Historical Landmark No. 141, for the "Hangman's Tree," is located on Main Street. Placerville is the county seat of El Dorado County. (Courtesy of Jon McCabe.)

The NSGW organized a celebration in Placerville for California's Admission Day. A parade was held on Main Street on September 9, 1898. The Lincoln Highway and later US Highway 50 ran through Placerville on Main Street. (Courtesy of Jon McCabe.)

Placerville had this sign put up outside of town over the southern route of the Lincoln Highway between Lake Tahoe and Sacramento. In 1927, named roads were numbered by the federal government, and this route became known as US Highway 50.

Rancho Cordova, in Sacramento County, was home to Mather Air Field, built in 1918. This is the entry gate to the airbase prior to World War II. Before closing in 1993, Mather was home to an operational wing of B-52s. Mather is now a private business area that includes a major medical center for veterans, a private airport, and a center for UPS cargo planes.

The Red Bluff "Sacramento Valley Loop" sign was erected in 1925 on US Highway 99 at the intersection of Main and Oak Streets. The 16-inch-high letters were lit on this sign that measured 20 feet wide and rose 18 feet above the roadway. It is unknown when the sign was removed. Red Bluff is the county seat of Tehama County.

The Richardson Springs Hotel, in Butte County, opened in 1903. This image of the entrance sign was taken in 1944. There are four different hot springs at the resort. It was named for brothers Joseph and Lee Richardson. The hotel was used to house soldiers during World War II. The CSAA sign in the photograph reads, "Cohasset Road 1 [Mile]" and "Butte Meadows 36 [Miles]."

The Rio Linda arch might look familiar, as it is one of seven such arches originally erected in Marysville in 1911. One of the Marysville arches was given free to Rio Linda in 1926. It was erected at Rio Linda Boulevard and M Street. Originally it had a small sign that said "Rio Linda," but it was eventually removed due to wind damage. The arch was renovated in 1985.

Riverton was originally on a toll road operated by John M. Moore. It was once called Moore's Station. The community is now registered as California Historical Landmark No. 705. It was a change station of the Pioneer Stage Company in the 1850s and 1860s. During 1860–1861, the Overland Pony Express maintained a pony remount station here. It is a small unincorporated community in El Dorado County.

Roseville, in Placer County, has two nearly identical arch signs constructed as part of the downtown and Vernon Street renovation project of 2002. Both are worded "Vernon Street" on one side and "Downtown Roseville" on the other side. The signs are steel, with a brick-faced base and backlit letters. This sign is on Vernon Street near Folsom Road.

Roseville's other sign over Vernon Street is near Pratt Road. Vernon Street was the historic route of the Lincoln Highway and US Highway 40. Roseville for many years was a major railroad town serving as the junction between west-east and south-north lines. In 1913, the largest ice manufacturing plant in the world opened in Roseville, where boxcars loaded with fruit were iced down for shipment east.

Rubicon Springs is located on the old Rubicon Trail, which dates to the 1860s. The small overhead wooden sign reads: "Welcome to Rubicon Springs—Elevation 6,110." The trail is now home to the Jeepers Jamboree, the world-famous test of off-road vehicles that has been held annually since 1952. The trail is an El Dorado and Placer County road easement that is an extremely popular and challenging four-wheel vehicle route.

A large, electrified arch was built in Sacramento to advertise Ruhstaller's Steam Beer around 1905. Sacramento had street fairs for many years in the early 20th century. Those fairs were known as Electric Carnivals and Floral Festivals. The first Grand Electric Carnival was held on September 9, 1895 (California Admission Day), when electric power first arrived in Sacramento from the Folsom Powerhouse and lit thousands of lightbulbs.

Sacramento's Oak Park sign was put up in 1903, when Sacramento Electric, Gas & Railway Company acquired the Oak Park terminus. This arch is possibly the earliest permanent welcome-type sign in California. Oak Park (now known as McClatchy Park) featured acres of shady oak trees in 1889 and, later, a wooden roller coaster, a roller-skating rink, an outdoor theater, and a scenic miniature railway.

The Oak Park land was purchased by the McClatchy family, which gave it to the city to become a city park named in honor of James McClatchy, the founder of the *Sacramento Bee* newspaper. The original Oak Park sign was gone by the 1930s. A new gateway arch, matching in design the original 1903 arch but at three-quarters size, was installed at the entrance to McClatchy Park in 2016.

This 1961 photograph shows the entrance to the old State Fair Grounds at Stockton Boulevard and Broadway in Sacramento. In 1968, the fair was relocated to the new Cal-Expo grounds on Exposition Boulevard.

Sacramento's Country Club Centre opened in 1952, which is probably about the time that this photograph of the overhead entrance sign was taken. It is located at the corner of El Camino Avenue and Watt Avenue. Country Club Centre was one of the earliest large shopping centers in the Sacramento area. A few active stores remain in 2021, but the entrance arch is long gone.

Sacramento's R Street illuminated steel arch sign was part of an effort to revitalize the area starting in 2002. Once a bustling warehouse district, the area's historic structures are now home to some of the best dining, entertainment, and arts centers in Sacramento. Sacramento has two other modern arch signs, one on Fulton Avenue and another at the entrance to the B.T. Collins US Army Reserve Center on Florin-Perkins Road.

The illuminated Strawberry sign dates from the 1930s. It hung over US Highway 50, formerly the Lincoln Highway's Sierra Nevada Southern Route. Strawberry is an unincorporated community on the South Fork American River in El Dorado County and a resort destination. It was a station along the Central Overland Pony Express route. It is now registered as California Historical Landmark No. 707.

Ukiah's illuminated hanging sign contained the slogan "Gateway to the Redwoods." The sign was over the old Redwood Highway, now US Highway 101, in the 1930s. Ukiah is the county seat and largest city of Mendocino County and is along the Russian River. It is a resort area that features, among other attractions, a redwood-tree service station built in 1936.

Another sign in downtown Ukiah is from a 1930s postcard. It directs traffic to the nearby Ukiah Valley Golf Course, opened in 1931. California Historical Landmark No. 980 in Ukiah is for the Vichy Springs Resort, established in the 1850s. It is one of the few continuously operating mineral springs in California and the only mineral springs in California that resembles the famed Grand Grille Springs of Vichy, France.

This arch at the entrance to Ukiah Municipal Park dates from 1919. The welcome message banner is probably for soldiers returning from World War I. Little else is known about this sign.

The Underwood Park entrance sign in 1949 is seen above. Underwood Park, formerly Coolidge Park, is on the Redwood Highway in northern Mendocino County. Nicknamed the "Drive-Thru Tree Park," it is a privately owned grove of coast redwoods that has been operated as a park by the Underwood family since 1922. The drive-through tree is 21 feet in diameter at its base, 315 feet high, according to its owner, and 2,500 years old.

The original Weed welcome arch was completed in 1922. It was at the intersection of Main Street and Weed Boulevard facing old US Highway 99. It was constructed of railroad rails and concrete. It was so sturdy that it took three weeks in 1963 to remove the structure.

A passenger bus is passing under the Weed arch in the 1940s. The city of Weed is in Siskiyou County and derives its name from Abner Weed, who in 1897 bought the Siskiyou Lumber and Mercantile Mill and 280 acres of land in what is now the city of Weed for only $400. (Courtesy of Vaune Dillman.)

The new Weed arch was erected over Main Street in 1990. The new sign is 63 feet wide, 16 feet high at the ends, and 24 feet tall in the center. It is decorated on both sides with a view of a snow-covered Mount Shasta. The new sign was a seven-year project spearheaded by Vaune and Barbra Dillman. Using mainly volunteer labor and donated materials, the sign cost $26,000. (Courtesy of Vaune Dillman.)

The photograph of the new sign perfectly frames Mount Shasta off in the distance. The sign is illuminated at night. Weed is about 10 miles west of Mount Shasta, which is the second-tallest volcano in the Cascade Range. The weed arch is so famous locally that it has its own beer, Weed Golden Ale, featuring the arch sign. (Photograph by Michael Lynch.)

The entrance arch to the Weimar Sanatorium was made of wood and stucco. It was right next to the route of old US Highway 40 at the time. The sanatorium opened on November 17, 1919, and it is thought that the arch dates from that time. A similar image of the entrance on a postcard is postmarked 1933. It is unknown when the arch was taken down. (Courtesy of Norm Sayler.)

The original Williams arch sign was dedicated in 1917 near the train station. The illuminated sign was renovated in 1985 and again in 2011. Williams was originally known as Central, with a post office established in 1874. The town and post office were renamed in 1876 in honor of William Williams. The city was incorporated in 1920. Williams is located on Interstate 5 and California Highway 20 in Colusa County.

The illuminated Willits arch, on US Highway 101, was donated to the city by Reno, Nevada, and dedicated in 1995. Willits has removed most of the original plastic panels and replaced the star with the US flag, and they switched the Reno slogan to "Heart of Mendocino County" on one side and "Gateway to the Redwoods" on the other. Willits is in Mendocino County.

This is what the Willits arch looked like when it was built in 1964 and erected in Reno, Nevada. This was the second version of such a welcoming sign in Reno, with this version costing around $100,000.

The slogan on the electrified overhead sign says "Glenn County Why? Irrigation," probably pointing out the importance of irrigation in the local agricultural industry. A parade proceeds down Main Street in Willows in the 1910s. Not shown but farther down the street is another overhead electric sign reading "Northern California Power Company," which was established in 1902. Another electric sign reading "Palace Hotel" also hung over Main Street in the 1920s. (Courtesy of Ed Schnurbusch.)

This welcoming sign was at the entrance to the town of Willows. The sign appears to be from the 1930s. Willows is the county seat of Glenn County. It was originally known as Willow until 1916, when the "s" was added to the name. The Willow Post Office opened in 1862.

This arch in Woodland was a temporary structure built to welcome the International Order of Odd Fellows (IOOF) grand encampment in 1909. It was in front of the Odd Fellows building on Main Street. The arch must have been in place in 1908, as that is the year this postcard image is postmarked. The city of Woodland is the county seat of Yolo County. (Courtesy of the Yolo County Historical Society.)

In 1917, a large electric sign was hung over the intersection of Miners Street and Main Street in Yreka, Siskiyou County. The lightbulb-lit letters were 26 inches tall. During the mid-1930s, Main Street (originally the Pacific Highway and later US Highway 99) was widened through town and the sign was taken down. The Art Deco sign was saved and remained at the city yard for more than 40 years.

In 1977, the Yreka sign was renovated and placed in a small park next to the freeway, where it can still be seen today. The renovations were done through the efforts of the Yreka chapter of the Soroptimist International. In 2019, the sign was again renovated with new wiring and LED lights. (Photograph by Michael Lynch.)

The Camp Lowe overhead entrance sign was on a single lane bridge that led across the Klamath River to the camp. The camp was located north of Yreka on old State Highway 99, at what is now the intersection of State Highway 96 and 263. Camp Lowe was developed by William and Laura Lowe and sold in 1929 to brothers Ivon and George Howard. The camp closed in 1948.

Two

SAN FRANCISCO BAY AREA
ALAMEDA, CONTRA COSTA, MARIN, NAPA, SAN MATEO, SANTA CLARA, SOLANO, SONOMA, AND SAN FRANCISCO COUNTIES

Pictured in 1935, this large directional lighted arrow sign points to the Antioch Bridge and Sacramento beyond. The small sign on top says "Victory Highway," which was one of the first designated transcontinental highways. The route is now California Highway 160. The original narrow 21-foot-wide Antioch Bridge was opened in 1926 and had a lift segment to allow ships to pass. It was replaced in 1978.

Berkeley had a welcome sign at the intersection of San Pablo Avenue and University Avenue around 1925. Under the sign is Lehigh streetcar no. 280 operating on the interurban Key System. The sign promotes the University of California and the "Manufacturing District." Berkeley, incorporated in 1878, is in Alameda County, and its western edge is right on San Francisco Bay.

Another view shows the Berkeley sign from the other side of the photograph above and years later. The sign now has an added section directing traffic to the Golden Gate Ferry, which was used to cross the bay prior to the Bay Bridge being built in 1936. The sign was taken down in 1942. (Courtesy of Berkeley Historical Society.)

The University of California, Berkeley, has a bronze-and-steel entrance sign that was erected in 1910 and still stands today. Named Sather Gate, it originally was at the end of Telegraph Avenue, which was also old US Highway 40. The gate is California Historical Landmark No. 946 and is listed in the National Register of Historic Places. Berkeley is the oldest University of California System campus, established in 1868.

Little is known about the Brentwood hanging sign. Based on this image, it was a typical sign with lighted letters from the 1930s. Brentwood is a Contra Costa County town serving as a San Francisco Bay Area bedroom community near Antioch. It incorporated in 1948. The historic sign is long gone, but Brentwood has a modern illuminated sign, erected in 2011.

The original Burlingame sign, built in 1922, had electric bulbs. It was over the El Camino Real highway (US Highway 101). It carried a message of "To Pacific City," an amusement park a few blocks away. The lightbulbs were changed to neon in 1937. In 1960, the letters were enlarged to 18 inches. It was refurbished again in 1988. This postcard is postmarked 1942. The sign still stands.

This is the only known image of the Byron lighted sign. Based on the vehicles in the image, the photograph was taken in the 1920s. Byron grew up around a Southern Pacific Railroad depot. It is an unincorporated community in Contra Costa County on California Highway 4. Historically, Byron was famous for the Byron Hot Springs, a resort in the early 1900s attracting movie stars and athletes.

The impressive Calistoga sign is from the 1930s and probably on California Highway 128. The illuminated letters on the sign say "The Gateway to Clear Lake," which lies north of the city on California Highway 29. The area is a major wine region in Napa County just north of the San Francisco Bay Area. The Napa Valley Railroad depot in Calistoga is registered Historic Landmark No. 687. (Courtesy of the California State Library.)

Camp Meeker, in Sonoma County, has had three different overhead signs, including a modern one that is still in place. Pictured is the second Camp Meeker sign, from the 1940s. The earliest sign was put up in the 1910s and was lettered "Camp Meeker" on one side and "Come Again" on the other. The Camp Meeker Volunteer Fire Department, whose fire trucks are in the picture, is still in existence.

The 1930s Concord sign was probably located in what is now the old downtown area. Two state highways still run through town, namely California Highway 4 and 242. Incorporated in 1905, Concord is in Contra Costa County.

Fairfield's electrified welcome sign identifies it as the county seat of Solano County. The vintage cars parked along the street indicate this is a 1940s photograph. The first Fairfield sign was installed in 1925, with the Lions Club footing the bill of $1,000. This sign is still over Texas Street, which was also US Highway 40 until Interstate 80 bypassed the city in the 1970s.

The Fairfield sign was completely refurbished in 1990. During refurbishing, it became known that there was a plan to relocate the sign. However, a 1,400-signature petition lobbied for keeping the sign at its original location. The petition was successful, and the refurbished sign is still on Texas Street.

In the 1990s, this was the overhead sign at the entrance gate to Travis Air Force Base. The base was originally named Fairfield-Suisun Army Air Base when construction began on it in 1942. The base was renamed in 1951 for Brig. Gen. Robert F. Travis. Travis Air Force Base handles more cargo and passenger traffic through its airport than any other military air terminal in the United States.

The Entrance to Armstrong Woods, Guerneville, Cal.

Guerneville is home to the Armstrong State Redwoods Natural Reserve. This Armstrong entrance sign dates from before 1917, when the park was privately owned and operated by the Col. James Armstrong family. Sonoma County purchased the land in 1917 and operated it as a county park until the state took over management of the land in 1934. Currently, the park preserves 805 acres of coast redwoods.

The image shows the Healdsburg lighted sign in 1936. The arrow-shaped sign, erected in 1927, directs travelers to the popular Russian River resorts. Reportedly, the sign was taken down in 1941. It was located at the intersection of West Street (Healdsburg Avenue) and Matheson Street on old US 101. Healdsburg is in Sonoma County and is home to three of the top wineries in the United States.

The Martinez sign was black with white letters traced with white neon. It is unknown when it was erected, but it was still up in 1937. In 2011, Martinez erected a new sign worded "Historic Downtown Martinez" on the Marina Vista Avenue entrance to old town off Interstate 680. Martinez is the seat for Contra Costa County. It sits at the southern end of the Benicia Bridge.

The Monte Rio Chamber of Commerce had this welcome sign erected in the 1940s. The sign is white with green letters and white neon. It sits over California Highway 116. There is a different message on each side of the sign. This westbound picture reads "Welcome to Monte Rio Vacation Wonderland." Monte Rio is located on the Russian River in Sonoma County. (Photograph by Michael Lynch.)

Eastbound travelers see the "Monte Rio Awaits Your Return" side of the sign. A California State Parks ranger patrol vehicle is passing under the sign. There are several state parks in the Russian River area. Monte Rio has been a popular vacation destination since the early 1900s. (Photograph by Michael Lynch.)

The 23-mile private Mount Diablo Scenic Boulevard toll road to the Mount Diablo peak was opened in 1915. Pictured is the Danville toll gate in the 1920s. Tolls were $1 per automobile (about $20 in 2021 dollars). The road and property on the summit were sold to California State Parks in 1921. Mount Diablo is 3,849 feet in elevation and is visible from most of the San Francisco Bay Area.

Mount Diablo became a state park in 1921, and the original arched toll station became the main park entrance with new signs. The park is now 20,000 acres in size. Land surveys of much of California and Nevada were located with reference to the intersection of longitude and latitude lines on the south peak of Mount Diablo. Mount Diablo is California Registered Historical Landmark No. 905.

The Ridgecrest Boulevard Toll Road to the top of Mount Tamalpais opened in 1925. It was constructed by private investors. Pictured is the sign at the Alpine toll gate. The road was taken over by the military in 1942. It was purchased by the state in 1948, along with 25 acres on the top of Mount Tamalpais, to become Mount Tamalpais State Park. Today, much of Mount Tamalpais is held by various public agencies.

The Napa State Asylum's rock entrance arch is seen on a postcard postmarked 1911. The psychiatric asylum opened in 1875 and was renamed Napa State Hospital in 1924. The 138-acre hospital was the second California state hospital after Stockton and is the oldest state hospital still operating. It sits next to California Highway 221. The rock arch no longer exists.

The 45-foot-wide Oakland arch sign on MacArthur Boulevard was dedicated on November 8, 2019. It was commissioned and funded by the Oakland Public Art Program. The arch was hand-painted and crafted by Eric Powell. The arch is located on the city's southern boundary. A similar arch, titled "Eastmont," is further along MacArthur Boulevard near Seventy-Third Avenue and was dedicated at the same time.

Jack London Square's overhead sign in Oakland is unique in that it crosses both a street and the Southern Pacific Railroad and Bay Area Rapid Transit (BART) tracks. There is another modern arch sign at the entrance to Jack London Square, a historic working waterfront and one of the Bay Area's well-known recreational, dining, and commercial districts. It contains the cabin where Jack London lived in the Klondike.

The relatively new entrance sign to Oakland International Airport is the first video display sign over a roadway identified by the authors. No doubt additional video over-roadways signs will be popping up in California. Oakland also has two other modern arch signs. The Laurel arch, dedicated in 2006, is on MacArthur Boulevard in the Laurel District. The other is an arch sign in the Fruitvale District.

Palo Alto is synonymous with the term "Silicon Valley." It is headquarters for a number of high-technology companies, including Hewlett-Packard, Space Systems/Loral, VMware, Tesla, Ford Research and Innovation Center, PARC, IDEO, Skype, Palantir Technologies, Houzz, and Lockheed Martin Advanced Technology Center. Parts of Stanford University's campus lies within the city limits. (Courtesy of Palo Alto Library.)

The electrically illuminated Pittsburg city sign was located at East Tenth Street and Railroad Avenue. It directed people to turn to reach the city's business district. In the picture are two CSAA-produced state route shield signs for California Highways 4 and 24. (Courtesy of the California State Library.)

Judging by the vehicles in the two pictures, the Pittsburg sign was up in the 1920s and 1930s. Citizens voted on the name "Pittsburg" on February 11, 1911, so the sign went up some time after that date. The name was selected to honor Pittsburgh, Pennsylvania, as the two cities shared a common steel-based industrial heritage.

Pleasanton's neon city sign was first lit in 1932 due to the efforts of the Pleasanton Women's Improvement Club. It was located on Main Street, which was also old California Highway 21. Two Plymouth police cars are parked in front of the police department on the left side of the image. A warning siren and lights were added to the sign in 1935. The sign is still at its original location at Main Street and Division Street.

A stone-and-wood arch marked the entrance to Aetna Springs Resort in Pope Valley in Napa County. The horseless carriage dates this photograph to the early 1900s. The resort had been a vacation destination since 1883. It closed in 1972. In 1987, the property was nominated to be added to the National Register of Historic Places. There are plans to restore the resort's historic structure.

Two nearly identical Redwood City signs, lit with incandescent bulbs, were put up in 1926. One was on El Camino Real (US Highway 101) at Broadway and the other on El Camino Real and Woodside Road. The sign's slogan, "Climate Best by Government Test," was the winning submission in a contest in 1925, facts notwithstanding. This photograph also shows a smaller "Dumbarton Bridge" panel with an arrow on it.

In this image of the Redwood City sign, the "Dumbarton Bridge" panel is gone. For a time, one of the signs carried a panel worded "San Mateo County Seat." In the early 1940s, neon lighting was added to the signs. By 1970, both signs were gone. A modern remake of the sign was erected in the 1990s. There is also a modern arch sign in the Theater District near Broadway and Arguello Street, erected around 2010.

The Richmond arch sign was erected in the 1920s on San Pablo Avenue (old US Highway 40) at McDonald Avenue. The sign had a steel frame and lighted lettering. By 1934, the panel on top of the sign had been removed. The small sign at left reads, "Golden Gate Ferry to S.F. Straight Ahead—Don't Turn Here." The arch was taken down in 1952. (Courtesy of the Richmond Museum of History.)

This is a modern, lighted steel entrance arch (completed in 2010) to Richmond's Point Potrero. The lettering on the sign says "Port of Richmond" and "Historic Richmond Shipyard Number Three." The medical program established in World War II for the shipyard workers at the Richmond Field Hospital eventually became today's Kaiser Permanente Health Maintenance Organization. On the sign is a plaque for California Historical Landmark No. 1032, Richmond Shipyards.

Dated 1864, this arch identifies the San Francisco Bay Shore and Fort Point Toll Road, which skirted the bay to reach the Army's Fort Point. This is the oldest known arch sign in California. The 1861 Fort Point is a national historic site sitting below the Golden Gate Bridge. This image is the entire stereoview from the renowned stereoview publishing firm of Lawrence & Houseworth.

A closeup scan of just one side of the stereoview shows more details, including the corner of the toll house at the left edge of the image and, in the background, Alcatraz Island in San Francisco Bay. The toll road was built by the Bay Shore and Fort Point Road Company, organized in 1863. The company incorporated with 2,000 shares at $100 each for a total of $200,000.

Soldiers are parading down San Francisco's Montgomery Street below an elaborate arch on July 4, 1865. This is the second oldest known arch in California. The arch is decorated with numerous US flags and images of Presidents Washington and Lincoln. This photograph was taken from the Austin Building. This was San Francisco's first July 4 celebration after the end of the Civil War in April 1865. (Courtesy of a private collector.)

Another temporary San Francisco welcome arch was installed at Market Street near Fourth Street. It was erected to welcome the 16th International Christian Endeavors Convention, being held in San Francisco from July 7 to July 12, 1897. San Francisco had at least 12 permanent and short-term ceremonial arches constructed between 1865 and 1925. (Courtesy of a private collector.)

What were probably the tallest and most grand arches ever constructed in California were those built for the 37th National Encampment of the Grand Army of the Republic (GAR) in San Francisco in 1903. These two massive, identical "GAR"-topped arches were erected on Market Street and connected by multiple strings of lights. Each arch was 77 feet high and 160 feet wide, and together, they were lit by more than 10,000 lightbulbs. A small portion of the second arch is at the far right in the image above. The photographs of the arches at night are fantastic. Tens of thousands marched, paraded, or just strolled under the impressive arches. The GAR was an organization of former soldiers of the Union army, navy, and marines who served in the American Civil War. The GAR was founded in 1866 in Springfield, Illinois, and grew to include hundreds of posts (local community units) across the nation. (Courtesy of a private collector.)

Ingleside Terrace had an elaborate stone-and-metal entrance arch when opened in 1912. Ingleside Terrace is an affluent historical San Francisco neighborhood. This main entrance sign was located at Junipero Serra Boulevard and Mercedes Way. The United Railroads streetcar line ran in front of the entrance arch. There were other arch entries to Ingleside Terrace, including at Victoria, Paloma, and Cedro Streets. (Courtesy of a private collector.)

San Francisco marked its southern city limits with this overhead lighted sign. The picture is dated 1928. The sign was located on San Bruno Avenue, now Bayshore Boulevard, at the intersection with Sunnydale Avenue, on old US Highway 101. This sign is unusual as it is the only known historic city limits sign hung up over a roadway. (Courtesy of Brian Smith.)

Two International Settlement arch signs were at either end of San Francisco's Barbary Coast, a red-light district on Pacific Avenue between Kearny and Montgomery Streets. Market Street Railway Streetcar No. 809 passes in front of the sign. The back of the sign was lettered "Thank You! Come Again." The arches lasted for about 20 years between the 1940s and 1960s. (Courtesy of a private collector.)

This dragon-style arch gate was erected along Bush Street at the intersection with Grant Avenue in 1970. The $75,000 arch was a gift from the Republic of China. San Francisco's Chinatown is claimed to be the oldest in North America and one of the largest Chinese enclaves outside of Asia. (Photograph by Sandor Balatoni.)

The San Mateo neon sign spanned old US 101. It points to the San Francisco Bay Toll Bridge (now the San Mateo–Hayward Bridge), which opened in 1929. Another image of the sign shows an additional panel that reads "East Bay Valley Points," probably added after the San Francisco–Oakland Bay Bridge opened in 1936. A replacement for the 1929 bridge opened in 1967.

The welcome sign in San Pablo, at the time of its construction in the early 2000s, was touted as the widest-span (at 110 feet) arch sign in California. It crosses San Pablo Boulevard (formerly Lincoln Highway and US Highway 40). Originally, the sign was lettered "San Pablo International Marketplace" for the shopping center at the site. The wording was changed to "Welcome to San Pablo" about 2009.

The Santa Rosa sign hung over Mendocino Avenue, the route through town for the Redwood Highway (US Highway 101). This photograph was taken from the Sonoma County Courthouse. Santa Rosa also had a NSGW parade arch, marked "Grace Bros Brewing Company" in large letters, in 1911. A modern steel arch sign is at the bus station. (Courtesy of the Sonoma County Library.)

The hanging Santa Rosa sign had a different message on each side. One side said "Santa Rosa," and the other said "Redwood Highway." This image is a still photograph from the Alfred Hitchcock movie *Shadow of a Doubt*, which was mostly filmed in Santa Rosa in August 1942. The movie starred Teresa Wright and Joseph Cotten. (Courtesy of the Sonoma County Library.)

Sunnyvale had this electrified sign installed in 1921 at what is today the intersection of El Camino Real (old US Highway 101) and Murphy Avenue. It was manufactured and installed by Hendy Iron Works using money provided by community contributors. The sign was taken down in 1942.

The Sunnyvale sign is shown down due to a windstorm in 1942. Sunnyvale has a modern lighted sign at the entrance to Murphy Avenue lettered "Historic Murphy Avenue." This was erected some time before 2011. (Courtesy of the Sunnyvale Historical Society and Museum Association.)

Built around 1915, a concrete overhead sign and bridge spanned Alamo Creek at the western entrance to Vacaville on the Lincoln Highway. When US Highway 40 was rerouted in 1935, the bridge and sign were demolished. Vacaville currently has a brightly colored, lighted arch sign reading "Downtown Vacaville" at the entrance to the historic downtown area. Two more modern arch signs are at the Nut Tree Center next to Interstate 80. (Courtesy of the Vacaville Heritage Council.)

This picture of the Vallejo overhead sign was taken in 1942. The sign contains the city slogan at the time, "The Naval City." The other wording on the sign, "Home of Mare Island Navy Yard," is superimposed on a barely visible naval ship. The sign was made by Cook Company. Vallejo is home to the California Maritime Academy and the former Mare Island Naval Shipyard, which closed in 1996.

The rustic-looking Woodacre arch sign is unique in that the letters are spelled out using actual tree branches and the structure is made mainly of tree limbs. Woodacre is a small unincorporated town in Marin County eight miles south-southwest of Novato and eight miles northwest of San Rafael. The community began when promoters subdivided the area in 1912.

The Veterans Home of California, founded in 1884 in Yountville, had a stone entrance arch in its early days. The arch no longer exists. The facility is the largest of its kind in the United States. Located in Napa County, it is California Historical Landmark No. 828. Near the entrance to the veterans home is a modern arch sign over California Drive leading to the Domaine-Chandon Winery.

Three

CENTRAL CALIFORNIA

ALPINE, CALAVERAS, FRESNO, INYO, KERN, KINGS, MADERA, MARIPOSA, MERCED, MONO, MONTEREY, SAN BENITO, SAN JOAQUIN, SAN LUIS OBISPO, SANTA CRUZ, STANISLAUS, TUOLUMNE, AND TULARE COUNTIES

Atascadero had a large, electrified banner-style sign in the 1930s across old US Highway 101. The sign remained in place up until the 1950s. The community was founded in 1913 by East Coast publisher Edward Gardner Lewis, who envisioned the place as a utopian planned colony. It was originally named Atascadero Colony. The town, in San Luis Obispo County, was incorporated in 1979.

The Bakersfield arched sign was built in 1949. The image is from a postcard postmarked 1955. The arch is an eight-foot-wide pedestrian walkway designed to link the two lobbies of the Bakersfield Inn, which were located on either side of Union Street. The large blue porcelain letters on the arch are neon lit and approximately five feet tall. The city is in Kern County.

The Bakersfield Inn suffered a long decline after US Highway 99 was realigned in the 1960s. In 1998, the arch was taken down. In 1999, a new sign was constructed using only the original blue porcelain letters salvaged from the original sign. The new sign was funded by singer-songwriter Buck Owens. It was placed next to the Buck Owens Crystal Palace on Sillect Avenue, where it stands today.

Big Basin Redwood State Park had two different overhead entrance signs. This is the sign at the main Boulder Creek entrance, which was erected in 1917. The sign reads, "State Redwood Park—To Be Preserved in a State of Nature." The sign was made of redwood logs. Pictured are members of the CCC working in the park in 1936. The sign was taken down in the 1950s.

The sign at the northern Skyline entrance to the Big Basin Redwood State Park was constructed in the 1920s. It read, "California Redwood Park—To Be Preserved in a State of Nature." The park was established in 1902. In 1950, the California Division of Highways (DOH) took over the park entrance road, which became California Highway 236. The sign was taken down by DOH in the 1950s.

The original Castroville sign was erected in 1931 over California Highway 1 on Merritt Street. It directed travelers to the Monterey Peninsula. The steel sign had neon letters. By the 1950s, the sign had been modified to read "The Artichoke Center of the World." Castroville, in Monterey County, was founded in 1863.

In 1991, the Castroville sign was completely renovated. The renovated sign is lit by overhead lights. A panel on the sign now promotes the Artichoke Festival, which was established in 1959. In 1948, Marilyn Monroe was crowned Castroville's California Artichoke Queen.

Chowchilla's illuminated sign was built by Orland Robertson to promote his townsite of 108,000 acres. The sign was dedicated in 1913 over Robertson Boulevard, which is now California Highway 233. The three-portal, Spanish-style arch had a span of 100 feet and cost $80,000. In the 1920s, the sign was reinforced with steel beams and cables. The Chowchilla Pacific Railway station was built in 1913 next to the arch.

A few years after it was constructed, the Chowchilla sign was updated to reflect the additional available land, which had increased the size of the townsite to 134,000 acres. This increase came when promoter Orland Robertson bought the Bliss Ranch. Robertson's company offered 40-acre plots for $250 per acre. The sign was destroyed by fire in 1937. Chowchilla is in Madera Country along State Highway 99.

The first Clovis sign was all wood and put up by the Clovis Chamber of Commerce in 1930. It was lit by small lightbulbs. In 1946, the original sign was replaced by a metal neon sign. The existing green-and-white neon "Gateway to the Sierras" sign was erected in 1951 on Clovis Avenue near Fifth Street on California Highway 168. The sign was refurbished in 1992.

The Exeter sign over California Highway 65 promoted that Exeter was the "Gateway to Sequoia National Park." For reasons unknown, the sign's concrete pillars were made to look somewhat like square redwood trees. The sign does not appear to be lighted. Exeter is in Tulare County.

The overhead entry sign to what is now Henry Cowell Redwoods State Park in Felton was probably erected in the 1930s. At the time, Santa Cruz County operated the area as Big Trees Park. In 1954, the county park was combined with another 1,600 adjoining acres donated by the Cowell family to become a state park. The state park is now more than 4,650 acres in size.

The original Fresno arch was built over Van Ness Boulevard at Railroad Street in 1917. The elaborate arch was constructed of terra cotta over a wooden framework. Floodlights illuminated the sign at night, and it had two flagpoles, one on each pillar. Van Ness Boulevard was the route of US Highway 99 through Fresno. This arch was destroyed by fire a few years after it was constructed.

A new Fresno arch, erected in 1925, carried the slogan "The Best Little City in the U.S.A." It was placed at the site of the 1917 arch. The new sign has neon letters. In 1980 and again in 2002, the sign was reconditioned, and it still stands today. Fresno has two other modern lighted metal arches reading "Downtown Fresno," one a double arch over a divided road.

Camp Mather, near Groveland, has a wooden arch sign at the entrance to the recreation camp owned and operated by the City and County of San Francisco since 1923. The area was originally a sawmill and housing area for the construction of the O'Shaughnessy Dam, built by San Francisco inside Yosemite National Park in the Hetch Hetchy Valley. A newer version of sign still stands with the slogan "Gateway to Hetch Hetchy."

The three interlinked rings on the welcome arch over Hollister's main street identify this as an Independent Order of Odd Fellows celebratory welcoming parade. The date of the sign is not known, but the clothing of the bystanders seems to indicate it is from the late part of the 19th century. The Odd Fellows did hold a large celebration in Hollister in 1884. Hollister is in San Benito County.

The entrance sign to the US Forest Service ranger station at Lee Vining is dated 1923. At the time, it was in Mono National Forest, but since 1945, it has been part of Inyo National Forest. Forest Service signs were made from porcelain enamel and usually had green letters on a white background. Early forests were required to have a single-word name, so Lee Vining became "Leevining" on the sign.

Lodi had two arches for the September 1907 Tokay Carnival, one permanent and one temporary. Both were over Pine Street in front of the Southern Pacific Railroad depot. In the background of this image is the temporary arch. An unobstructed view of the temporary arch is on page 6. In the foreground, in the final stages of construction, is the permanent arch, which still exists today. (Courtesy of the California State Library.)

The Lodi arch is a 34-foot-tall, 42-foot-wide structure over the roadway and has a total width of 80 feet. It is one of the few remaining Mission Revival ceremonial structures within California and is California Historical Landmark No. 931. In 1910, a papier-mâché bear was added to the arch facing south. The sign and bear were remodeled in 1956, when the bear was turned to face north.

The current Lodi arch did not originally have the word "Lodi" on it. The lighted letters were added some time after 1908. The initial slogan slated for the arch was "Lodi—The Home of the Tokays." The Mission Revival–style arch was designed by Lodi architect E.B. Brown. In 1980, the arch was officially added to the National Register of Historical Places. (Photograph by Michael Lynch.)

Lodi also has a modern gateway arch in the downtown area over School Street. It was constructed using funding from the Central City Revitalization Improvement Project and was completed in 1998. (Photograph by Michael Lynch.)

Manteca had two versions of lightbulb-lit signs over Yosemite Avenue (US Highway 99). Prior to 1915, one version of the sign, as pictured here, had only lit letters with no background. The other version of the sign had a background behind the letters. Manteca is in San Joaquin County.

Merced had two different arch signs, one at each end of town over Sixteenth Street, old US Highway 99 at the time. The two-foot-wider V Street arch is pictured on page 2. Both signs carried the same "Gateway to Yosemite" slogan. This arch, near G Street, straddled a concrete bridge. The sign, taken down in the 1950s, was made of concrete with neon-lit black-and-white letters.

Modesto, in Stanislaus County, has what is considered the oldest slogan arch sign in the United States. The slogan was adopted based a public contest. The 70-foot-wide arch was dedicated in 1912 and had a small "Welcome" sign attached to it, which lasted only two years. The $2,500 cost of the sign was raised by the public. This photograph was taken in 1918. The stone pillars were renovated in 1934.

A postcard shows the Modesto arch during the city's centennial in 1954. The arch was at Ninth and I Streets next to the train station. It was originally electrified with 384 incandescent lightbulbs on each side, which were very costly to electrify and maintain. In 2012, the arch underwent a major refurbishment, including adding LED lights. The sign is nicknamed "Prosperity Arch."

The US Army Presidio of Monterey arch is pictured here in the 1930s and was still in place in 1945. It was one of two historical arch signs at the presidio. There is currently a modern wooden arch sign at the Artillery Gate. The presidio has been a US military installation since 1846. It is an active Army installation that is the home of the Defense Language Institute–Foreign Language Center.

The "Saludes Amigos" arch sign was over Alvarado Street in Monterey in 1949 for the centennial of California's constitutional convention of 1849. The street was painted gold for the celebration. Although many California communities have Spanish names, this is the only known Spanish-language overhead slogan sign in California. (Photograph by Rey Ruppel.)

Probably in the 1930s, this simple arch banner-style sign in Oakdale was hung over F Street, the main street through town and the route of California Highway 120. Oakdale, in Stanislaus County, is in the San Joaquin Valley just northeast of Modesto.

Oakdale had a new sign erected in same spot as the original sign. The slogan on the sign reflected the slogan of the city during the 1940s. The city once had a slogan of "Gateway to Yosemite," which did not make it on the sign. The city's current slogan is "Cowboy Capital of the World."

The 1950s overhead Pismo State Beach sign highlighted the laws regarding digging for the famous Pismo clam, now nearly extinct. The overhead sign was over the vehicle entrance ramp onto the beach on Grand Avenue near California Highway 1. Motorized vehicles have used the beach since 1906. Established in 1934, the expanded park was separated in 1974 into Pismo State Beach and the Oceano State Vehicular Recreation Area.

The Point Pinos Lighthouse, in Pacific Grove, is framed in this wooden overhead entrance sign. A modern replica of this sign is over the service road and pedestrian entry to the lighthouse. The lighthouse was first lit in 1855. It is the oldest continuously operating lighthouse on the West Coast and still uses its original lens to reflect the light. It is an active Coast Guard station.

The Paso Robles Hotel sign was over Spring Street, which was also the old route of US Highway 101. The hotel opened for business in 1891. It was three stories tall and spread out over three continuous blocks. Inside the hotel was a library, a beauty salon, a barbershop, hot springs baths, and various lounging rooms. This probably explains why the word "hotel" is featured on the town's sign.

The Pixley Women's Club paid for the electrified Pixley sign in 1927. It was over Main Street, which was US Highway 99 at the time. The sign was opposite the Artesia Hotel, constructed in the late 1890s. The hotel was named after the artesian wells that were common to the area. The sign was taken down when a law was passed banning signs hanging over a main traveled road.

The earliest Salinas sign was erected in the early 1920s on Main Street. The lettering below the word "Salinas" read "Chamber of Commerce—California Rodeo," with an arrow reading "Stop for Information." By 1929, the wording was "Chamber of Commerce—Information," and a cowboy hat had been added. Next, the sign read "Home of California Rodeo." From 1937 to 1942, the sign read "California Rodeo" with the year of the rodeo.

This Salinas sign was over Main Street on old US Highway 101. All the versions of the Salinas sign were illuminated. By the 1950s, images of Main Street no longer show the sign. Salinas, in Monterey County, has four modern overhead signs, one on the railroad bridge over Main Street, another on Monterey Street, another at the Amtrak station, and one going into the historic Boronda District.

Santa Cruz had a temporary parade arch erected by the NSGW, most probably for the huge 1891 Admissions Day (September 9) parade event held in the city. Also in 1891, a granite archway, funded by public subscriptions, was dedicated in front of the mission church to commemorate the founding of Mission Santa Cruz. The mission is California Historical Landmark No. 342.

Santa Cruz had a welcome arch sign by the 1920s on Plymouth Street (old California Highway 17). One must wonder about the meaning of the slogan "Santa Cruz Never Closes" on the sign. A small sign on the left of the image says "City Limit." Little else is known about this sign. Santa Cruz is the county seat of Santa Cruz County.

This is the main gate of the US Army's Fort Ord off California Highway 1 near Seaside. The 7th Infantry Division was stationed there from 1974 until the base was closed in 1994. After the closure, the gate was taken down. Most of the former base became Fort Ord National Monument, and other portions are now California State University, Monterey Bay, and Fort Ord Dunes State Park.

The entrance sign to Sequoia National Park was on Colony Mill Road 10 miles north of Three Rivers in 1920s. The small sign reads "North Fork Entrance." The name of the town of Three Rivers comes from its location near the junction of the North, Middle, and South Forks of the Kaweah River. Sequoia National Park was established in 1890, and in 1943, it was combined administratively with Kings Canyon National Park.

The Sonora and Mono Toll Road operated from 1864 to 1901, when it was bought out by the state to eventually become California Highway 108. The toll road was well used when the mining town of Bodie was booming in 1877. It had stops at Sugar Pine, Strawberry, Baker's Station, Levitt's Station, and Big Meadows and ended in Bridgeport. The Sonora and Mono Toll Road is California Landmark No. 422.

Sonora Pass was at one time marked by this simple pipe-mounted overhead sign. From the vehicle and the unpaved roadway, the picture is probably from the late 1920s or early 1930s. Sonora Pass is 9,624 feet in elevation, making it the second highest highway pass crossing the Sierra Nevada. The pass is near the boundaries of Tuolumne, Alpine, and Mono Counties.

In 1927, the local American Legion purchased this site for a permanent Stanislaus County fairground in Turlock, thus the "Legion Field" wording on the arch. For three months in 1942, the fairground was used as an assembly center for Japanese Americans being relocated to more permanent concentration camps. From 1942 to 1945, it was an Army rehabilitation center for soldiers, and the arch sign read "Rehabilitation Center—Ninth Service Command."

The wording on the entrance sign was changed to "Stanislaus County Fair" in 1956. In 1999, the fair arch gate was recognized by the board of supervisors as a point of historical interest, and a marker was unveiled at the 1999 fair that is on public display inside the arch gate. The fairground is also California Historical Landmark No. 934, recognizing its use as a World War II detention center.

The original Twain Harte arch sign was erected in the late 1920s using logs and tree limbs. It is shown here with a Twain Harte fire truck. There were four versions of the Twain Harte arch sign. All were at the junction of Joaquin Gulley Road and California Highway 108. The second sign was a similar log sign with cables to support the two-foot-high letters. It was erected in the 1930s.

This image is of Twain Harte's third arch sign, built about 1946. The existing forth version of the Twain Harte arch is a stone-and-wood structure with overhead lighting built in 1986 and renovated in 1992. Twain Harte was named after Mark Twain and Brett Harte, two famous authors who once lived in California. Twain Harte is in Tuolumne County.

World-famous Yosemite National Park had an arch sign at the entrance to the Mariposa Grove of Big Trees section of the park in the 1920s. The sign was most likely porcelain enamel with green letters on a white background, a common design used by the National Park Service at that time. Yosemite had another, more elaborate log sign at the Wawona Entrance to the park, also in the 1920s.

Yosemite National Park's Camp Curry, in Yosemite Valley, had a rustic wood welcome entrance sign constructed in 1914 by Foster Curry. Originally over the entrance road, the renovated sign is now over a pedestrian walkway in front of Curry Village. The Camp Curry letters are now lit by small lightbulbs. Camp Curry first opened in 1899, when Yosemite Valley was a California state park.

Four

SOUTHERN CALIFORNIA
IMPERIAL, LOS ANGELES, ORANGE, RIVERSIDE, SAN
BERNARDINO, SAN DIEGO, SANTA BARBARA, AND
VENTURA COUNTIES

The Alhambra sign had letters at least two feet high that were lit by individual lightbulbs. Judging by the cars in the image, the sign was in place in the 1930s. In the 1940s, Alhambra added three neon welcome signs based on the design of the overhead sign, but these three replicas were alongside the main roads into the city, not overhead. Neon signs were first introduced in the United States in the early 1920s by Georges Claude and his French company Claude Neon.

This image of the overhead entrance sign to Disneyland's parking was probably taken not long after it opened in 1955 in Anaheim. The smaller sign on the pillar states that parking is 25¢, which was the fee charged when Disneyland opened. In 2021, the Disneyland parking fee was $20 per vehicle. As of 2018, Disneyland has a larger cumulative attendance than any other theme park in the world, with 726 million visits.

Arcadia had two overhead signs put up in the 1930s. This 1947 photograph was taken of men under the Arcadia sign at the intersection of First Avenue and Huntington Drive. There was an identical sign over Duarte Road. There is a modern painted Arcadia sign on the railroad bridge on the route of old US Highway 66, which went through Arcadia. (Courtesy of Arcadia City Library.)

The lighted Banning sign was up in the 1930s through 1940s. It spanned old US Highway 99 on Ramsey Street. Small lettering on the sign read "For Health" and "Elevation 2320," Banning is located about 90 miles east of Los Angeles in Riverside County.

To the right of the Banning sign in this image is the Del Paso Hotel, which opened in 1924 at the northwest corner of Ramsey Street and San Gorgonio Avenue. Banning was incorporated in 1913. The town was named after Phineas Banning, who had an honorific title of brigadier general bestowed upon him to recognize the support he provided to the Union cause in Southern California during the Civil War.

Big Pines Park had three historic overhead signs. Originally named Big Pine Park, this was the first entrance sign to the park, which was dedicated in 1924. The park name was changed to Big Pines in 1926. The area was developed as a recreational site by Los Angeles County. The first woman park ranger, Dorothy Hillabrand, was appointed in 1926. The area is in Angeles National Forest in the San Gabriel Mountains.

A more extensive rock pillar arch entrance sign was constructed in 1927. This sign now reads "County of Los Angeles—Big Pines Recreation Camp." The sign alongside the road is a US Forest Service sign stating "Help Prevent Fires." During the 1930s, Los Angeles County had difficulty funding the park, and it was taken over by the US Forest Service in 1941. (Courtesy of Pomona Public Library.)

Located near the Big Pines ranger station and lodge was an extensive rock arch with a date on it of 1926. The arch was designed and erected by William Davidson and donated to the county. There are photographs of the arch up until 1949. It may have been taken down in 1956, when California Highway 2 was completed through the area. The tower of the arch on the left still stands today.

The Blythe California Agricultural Station went into use when Interstate 10 was completed in 1972. The mission-style station even has a mission-style bell on top of the structure. The previous inspection station also had an overhead sign and was on old US Highway 60 west of the border with Arizona. Blyth is in Riverside County.

The "Brea Welcomes You" sign was funded by the Brea Lions Club and dedicated in 1934. The sign, 3 feet by 10 feet, was black and white with white-and-gold neon-lit letters. It was on Pomona Avenue, now Brea Boulevard. The sign was taken down in 1992, when a vehicle damaged one of the pillars. The sign was renovated in 2001 and placed on a pole alongside Brea Boulevard.

There were four neon Burbank signs, all the same, at various roads entering Burbank: on San Fernando Road, Magnolia Boulevard, Victory Boulevard, and Barham Boulevard. The signs went up in the 1930s, and some were still up in the 1960s. Burbank has long been a movie- and TV-oriented town. It is located about 12 miles northwest of downtown Los Angeles.

At the Calexico border crossing with Mexico, there was a large two-sided overhead sign in the 1920s. One side of the sign said "United States" and the other side "Mexico." The overhead sign at the border was still in place in 1950 but gone soon thereafter. A similar sign was on the border at the San Ysidro crossing into Mexico. Calexico is in Imperial County.

Looking from the US side, the Calexico overhead border sign says "Mexico." On the right side of the image is a sign marking the southern end of US Highway 99, which, until it was replaced by Interstate 5 in 1972, ran from Calexico to the Canadian border at Blaine, Washington. Calexico is linked economically with the much larger city of Mexicali, the capital of the Mexican state of Baja California.

The entrance road into the ghost town of Calico had this overhead sign. The ghost town is now a San Bernardino County regional park and California Historical Landmark No. 782. (Photograph by Merle Porter.)

This sign was for the Eichbaum Death Valley Toll Road. In 1926, Herman William Eichbaum obtained a franchise for a 35-mile toll road from Darwin Falls to Stovepipe Wells. It was the first maintained road into Death Valley from the west. It changed the area's economic base to tourism and brought about the creation of Death Valley National Monument in 1933. The road is California Historical Landmark No. 848.

The backside of the Death Valley Toll Road sign was worded "Mt Whitney Toll Road," apparently to promote the tourist potential for the road. The creation of Death Valley National Monument in 1933 hastened the end of Eichbaum's toll road, and in 1934, his estate sold the toll road to the State of California. Initially designated California Highway 127, it was redesignated California Highway 190 in 1964.

The entrance to the Furnace Creek Ranch resort had this arch sign in the 1950s. The sign has varied over the years, and it is still in place. The resort is next to California Highway 190 in Death Valley National Park. The Pacific Coast Borax Company built the resort in 1927 in an elegant Spanish architectural style. The resort is now named Ranch at Death Valley.

The lighted 1930s El Monte sign stated it was "The End of the Spanish Trail," though historically the trail ended at Mission San Gabriel six miles farther west. The Old Spanish Trail ran from Santa Fe, New Mexico, starting in 1829. In 2002, this trail was designated as part of the National Trails System. El Monte also has a modern overhead sign painted in large letters on an overpass bridge.

This view of the Encinitas sign is from a postcard captioned "Highway 101, the Great American Road." The sign from the 1930s was lit with neon. Encinitas is a beach city in the northern part of San Diego County, approximately 25 miles north of the city of San Diego, with Interstate 5 going through the city's western section.

This modern arch sign in Encinitas appears to have used a renovated original sign or is a new sign based on the original sign. It is on South Coast Highway 101 near D Street, on the historic route of US 101 through Encinitas. The image was taken at night. (Photograph by Michael James Slattery.)

The Escondido sign may be the widest span arch in California at 180 feet. The first lighting and the dedication of the sign was on March 23, 2020. The 40-foot-high arch was designed by Moore Ruble Yudell. Funding for the arch was raised by the Escondido Charitable Foundation, mainly from a very generous $1-million anonymous donation.

In 1937, this "Fullerton Come Again" message was painted on the old Pacific Electric Railway bridge over Spadra Road (now Harbor Boulevard) in Fullerton. The Pacific Electric Railway Company was a privately owned mass transit system in Southern California consisting of electrically powered streetcars and interurban cars. It was the largest electric railway system in the world in the 1920s. Fullerton is in Orange County.

Glendora's lighted overhead sign spelled out the city slogan, "The Pride of the Foothills." The slogan is still used today and dates back to 1930s. Glendora is about 26 miles east of Los Angeles in Los Angeles County. It is known for being nestled in the foothills of the San Gabriel Mountains, thus the city's slogan. Old US Route 66 ran through Glendora.

Huntington Beach's sign is being hoisted into place in the early 1930s. It was over Main Street and the Pacific Coast Highway (old US Highway 101). It was strung under four arch pillars, arching over the middle of the roadway from each corner of the intersection. Huntington Beach is a seaside community in Orange County. It is known for its 9.5-mile-long stretch of sandy beach.

The Huntington Beach sign is now in place. It was lighted at night and had a streetlight at the bottom of the sign. Some time in the 1940s, the hanging lettered portion of the sign was removed, leaving only the lighted arches. In 1905, Huntington Beach also had a "Welcome to Huntington Beach" banner sign over Main Street.

This is the lighted Indio sign, probably in 1937. The city of Indio is in the Coachella Valley in Riverside County. Old US Highways 60, 70, and 99 all ran through Indio. It lies 23 miles east of Palm Springs and 127 miles east of Los Angeles. Indio used to be known as the "Hub of the Valley" and at one time had the slogan "The Place to Be." (Courtesy of Brian Smith.)

The lighted Laguna Beach sign hung on Ocean Avenue in the downtown area over what in the 1940s was designated US Highway 101 Alternate. Laguna Beach, in Orange County, is another one of Southern California's many seaside communities.

The entrance to Long Beach Naval Shipyard had a large overhead sign. The shipyard operated from 1940 to its closure in 1997. The primary role of the shipyard at the time of its closure was the overhaul and maintenance of conventionally powered Navy surface ships. Coauthor Art Sommers was stationed at this naval shipyard in 1973, when his ship the USS *Hepburn* (DE-1055) was homeported at Long Beach.

This elaborate arch sign was for the arrival of the Los Angeles Cable Railway to the Boyle Heights community in 1889. The cable railway tracks were laid down on First Street. The cable railroad was the first mechanical street railway in Los Angeles when it opened in 1885. The Boyle Heights neighborhood is east of downtown Los Angeles on the east bank of the Los Angeles River.

This 1908 photograph is of a temporary welcome arch at Harbor City. It would have been just before San Pedro and Harbor City were annexed in 1909 by the City of Los Angeles, making the port an official part of Los Angeles.

A postcard postmarked 1907 shows a miniature railway below the lighted hanging Venice sign. The sign hung over Windward Avenue at Pacific Avenue. The sign was probably part of the Venice of America development, which opened on July 4, 1905. The sign still exists today. Venice is known for its canals, a beach, and Ocean Front Walk, a two-and-a-half-mile pedestrian promenade that features performers, fortune tellers, artists, and vendors.

In 1938, Los Angeles's Chinese community gathered to dedicate the West Gate to celebrate the opening of New Chinatown (its original location, about a mile away, was demolished to make room for Union Station). The gate was on Gin Ling Way at North Hill Street. California governor Frank F. Merriam presented a plaque dedicated to the builders. The city declared the gate a historic cultural monument in 2005.

A modern Chinatown overhead gateway was erected in 2001. Officially, it is the Chinatown Gateway Monument, but it is also known as the "Dragon Gate." It spans North Broadway Avenue. The tops of the gatekeeper dragons' heads soar 43 feet above the ground and are set on 80-foot-wide steel trusses. The gateway was designed by Chinese-born architect Ruppert Mok. Note the Historic US Route 66 sign in the image.

This image shows what is known as the Melrose Gate entrance to the Paramount movie studio in Hollywood. The Paramount Pictures Corporation is a world-famous American film production and distribution company. It is the second oldest film studio in the United States (behind Universal Pictures) and the sole member of the "Big Five" film studios still located within the city limits of Los Angeles.

This artist's rendering is of an arch gateway sign scheduled for construction in the near future to recognize the entrance to Filipinotown. Filipinotown was designated an official historic Los Angeles neighborhood in 2002. The Los Angeles area is home to over half a million Filipinos, the largest population outside the Philippines. The gateway was described by the city as "a permanent reminder that showcases the beauty and storied history of the Filipino community."

Dated 1956, this is Lynwood's lighted overhead sign from a postcard. Given the size of the street in the image, it was probably on old California Highway 15, which passed through the city in the 1950s. Lynwood, in Los Angeles County, was incorporated in 1921. The name of the city is derived from Lynn Wood Sessions, the wife of a local dairy farmer.

The lighted Monterey Park sign was at the intersection of Garvey Avenue and Garfield Avenue in the old downtown section of the city, probably in the 1930s. Former US Highways 60, 70, and 99 all passed through Monterey Park. In 1926, Laura Scudder invented the first sealed bag of potato chips in Monterey Park. Laura Scudder's potato chips filled 50 percent of the California market in 1957.

The banner strung below the illuminated National City sign is referring to the Olympic Games held in Los Angeles in 1932. The sign was probably on National City Boulevard, the main street through the old downtown and the route of former US Highway 101. National City has a modern overhead sign spanning National City Boulevard.

This image of Ontario's lighted city sign looks like it was taken in the 1920s. There is a slogan below the main lettering, but it is unreadable in this postcard view. Old US Highways 70 and 99 passed through Ontario. The city has designated 95 structures and properties as historic landmarks. It takes its name from the Ontario Model Colony development, established in 1882.

In 1926, this Hollywood by the Sea sign was the entrance to an 80-acre Oxnard ranch developed by Fred J. Cutting, who leveled the dunes and carved out 100 small individual lots. He christened the site "Hollywood by the Sea," even though Hollywood was 50 miles away. The new development had a five-acre lake and 40-room hotel and promoted camping and picnicking on the beach.

An old lithograph postcard printed in Germany shows a gate into Westmoreland Place, a Pasadena neighborhood. The location was originally a block-long private gated community around 1912. Westmoreland Place was sometimes chosen as a place to build homes by the rich to avoid "millionaire's row" on South Orange Grove Street in Pasadena.

This illuminated Riverside sign was on the Rubidoux Bridge, built across the Santa Ana River to West Riverside in 1928. The bridge is also known as the "Mission Bridge" because of its Spanish mission-style architecture. The sign was gone before the bridge was replaced in 1953. There was a different version of the Riverside sign on the opposite end of the bridge at one time.

From a postcard, this image shows another Riverside sign on a wide boulevard, probably old US Highway 60 or 395, which ran through Riverside before the new freeway system was constructed. Another arch in Riverside was built in 1895 for an enormous Orange Day celebration. The *Los Angeles Times* described the celebration as "the greatest day in the history of Riverside."

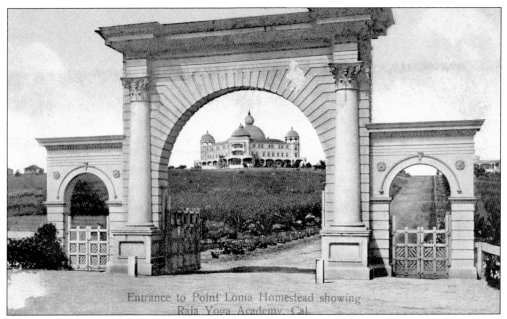

Entrance to Point Loma Homestead showing
Raja Yoga Academy, Cal.

Point Loma is a seaside community within the city of San Diego. Katherine Tingley moved the headquarters of the Theosophical Society to Lomaland, a hilltop campus in Point Loma overlooking the ocean, in 1900. The facility, with its unusual architecture and even more unusual lifestyles, became an important inspiration of music and culture for residents of San Diego until it closed in 1942.

MAIN ENTRANCE, U. S. NAVAL TRAINING STATION, SAN DIEGO, CALIFORNIA—24

The naval training center in San Diego was where Navy recruits went to boot camp. It was open from 1923 to 1997. The site is listed in the National Register of Historic Places, and many of the individual structures are designated as historic by the City of San Diego. The base was selected for closure by the Base Realignment and Closure Commission at the end of the Cold War. It is now the site of Liberty Station, a mixed-use community being redeveloped and repurposed by the City of San Diego.

This is the arch entry to the Del Mar Heights area, a housing development first promoted in 1913. As there are no houses yet built, it can be concluded that the picture was taken in 1913. The area is now an upscale neighborhood sandwiched between the coast and Interstate 5 in the northern part of the city of San Diego. (Courtesy of San Diego History Center.)

San Diego's historic Mahoney Airport entrance arch sign proclaimed, "Where Lindbergh Started." The photograph was taken in 1927, when Mahoney was a small commercial airport located at 3200 Barnett Avenue, directly opposite a marine barracks. The field was said to have a 2,500-foot northwest/southeast runway and a 1,400-foot northeast/southwest runway. In 1929, the field was the terminus for Maddux Air Lines and Pickwick Airways.

An Art Deco–style metal-and-neon Hillcrest sign was sponsored by the Women's Business Association and erected in 1940 over University Avenue at Fifth Avenue in San Diego. The sign deteriorated over the years, and a 1984 fundraising drive took in $4,000 to refurbish the sign, which still exists today.

East San Diego's illuminated overhead sign was in place from 1930 to the 1970s. This picture was taken about 1967. The sign was located on the corner of Fairmount Avenue and University Avenue. East San Diego was an independent city from 1912 to 1923, when it was annexed by the City of San Diego.

The "Normal" in this Normal Heights sign refers to the State Normal School in San Diego. The sign on Adams Avenue at Felton Street was put up in 1951 for $2,500 and renovated in 1983. Normal schools were also known as teachers' colleges. The normal school was in the adjacent University Heights neighborhood and was founded in 1899.

The Kensington sign in the city of San Diego was put up in 1956 over Adams Avenue at a cost of $1,900. The blue-and-white sign had large white letters traced with white neon tubing. It was designated a City Historical Resources Board historic site. In 1990, the original sign was meant to be renovated, but mistakes were made, and a new replica sign was erected in 2010.

North Park, in the city of San Diego, has had three different overhead signs. The first one, in place from 1925 to 1928, carried the slogan "Home of the Famous Toyland Parade." The sign pictured here was erected in 1932 and had white neon-outlined letters on a green background. This sign lasted until 1967. An exact replica sign was erected in 1993 over University Avenue.

San Diego's Little Italy sign was lit in October 2000. It commemorates the historical Italian neighborhood that was the hub of the world's tuna fishing and canning industry up until the 1960s. The sign was created by the Little Italy Design Committee. The airliner flying below the arch demonstrates why San Diego's Lindbergh Airport has been rated by pilots as the fifth worst in the country.

The city of San Jacinto had an overhead electrified sign in the 1930s. From this and other images of the sign, it was probably on Main Street, which would have been California Highway 79 at the time. It appears to have been taken down in the 1950s, as pictures of Main Street in the 1950s do not show the sign. San Jacinto is in Riverside County.

Soldiers are marching under the overhead Santa Ana Army Air Base sign during World War II. The main entrance to the base was at Newport Boulevard. The base was activated in February 1942 and deactivated in March 1946. It was a pre-flight-training base with no planes, hangars, or runways. The base was under the jurisdiction of the West Coast Army Air Corps Training Command Center, located in Santa Ana.

The Santa Ana arch sign was over the former US Highway 101 looking south from Chapman Avenue. It read "Direct Route—Santa Ana and Coast Cities." Santa Ana has a modern replica arch sign dedicated in 2007. On South Main Street near Warner Avenue, the new sign reads "Historic South Main Business District." It cost $300,000 to build. Santa Ana is the county seat of Orange County.

The Santa Ana arch, pictured here about 1930, was next to the Orange County Hospital, which was constructed in 1914. The back of the sign stated, "You are leaving Santa Ana—U.S. 101—Anaheim 4 Mi.—Fullerton 7 Mi.—Whittier 21 Mi.—Los Angeles 34 Mi." This would seem to indicate that the sign was on the northern city limit.

Ocean Park is a neighborhood in the city of Santa Monica in Los Angeles County. The neighborhood was home to a 28-acre, nautical-themed amusement park built on a pier at Pier Avenue. The park was intended to compete with Disneyland. The park opened in 1958 and closed in 1967. This image is from an early-1920s postcard and is looking down Pier Avenue years before the amusement park opened.

The famous Santa Monica Pier sign was officially unveiled in 1941. The sign was built by the Pan-Pacific Neon Sign Company for $2,000. The sign is approximately 20 feet high and 35 feet wide. A small sign at the arch marks the traditional end of old US Highway 66. The city owns the sign and in 2012 designated it as Santa Monica City Historic Landmark No. 98.

Santa's Village, at Skyforest in San Bernardino County, had an overhead sign. The amusement park opened in May 1955. The 230-acre park was one of Southern California's biggest tourist attractions. It had kiddie rides, a bobsled, a monorail, and a Ferris wheel. It also had a petting zoo, live reindeer, and shops including a bakery, candy kitchen, and toy shop. Santa's Village closed in 1998.

This postcard image of the Upland sign is looking down Euclid Avenue. Upland was on the National Old Trails Road, established in 1912 as the first national coast-to-coast highway. In Upland, it ran along Foothill Boulevard. In 1926, the National Old Trails Road became the famed US Highway 66 (better known as Route 66). An existing modern version of the Upland sign has the wording "Historic Downtown Upland."

INDEX

Asterisks indicate locations with existing signs in 2021.

Discover Thousands of Local History Books
Featuring Millions of Vintage Images

Arcadia Publishing, the leading local history publisher in the United States, is committed to making history accessible and meaningful through publishing books that celebrate and preserve the heritage of America's people and places.

Find more books like this at
www.arcadiapublishing.com

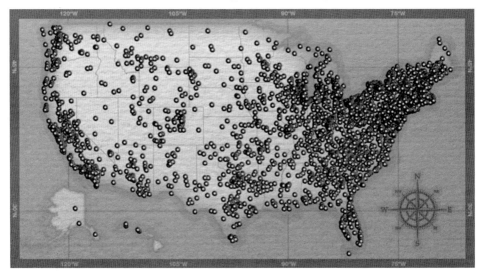

Search for your hometown history, your old stomping grounds, and even your favorite sports team.